EGYPT

Ancient Traditions, Modern Hopes

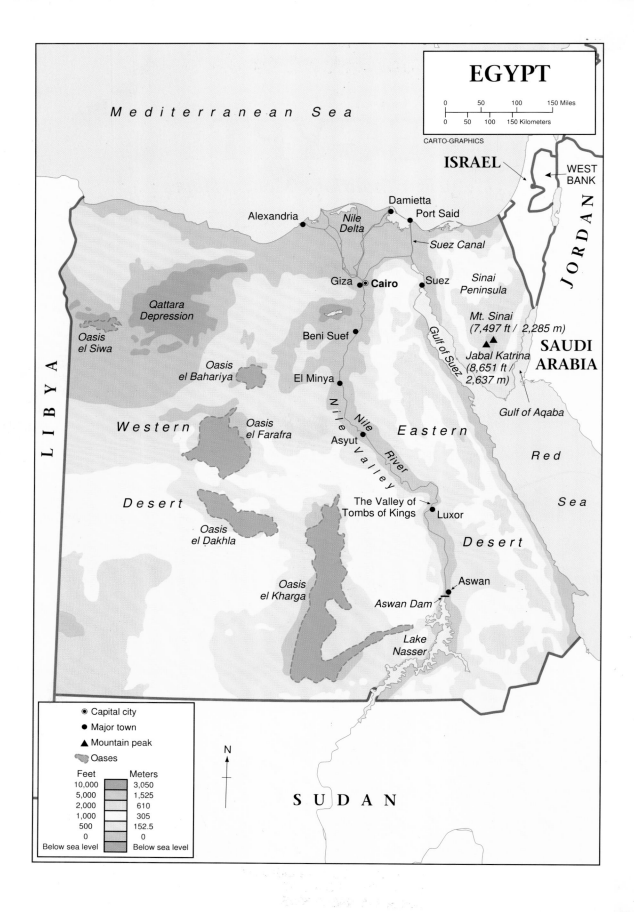

EXPLORING CULTURES OF THE WORLD

EGYPT

Ancient Traditions, Modern Hopes

David C. King

BENCHMARK BOOKS

MARSHALL CAVENDISH

NEW YORK

With thanks to Elsa Marston, writer and scholar in Middle Eastern affairs, for her expert review of the manuscript.

Benchmark Books
Marshall Cavendish Corporation
99 White Plains Road
Tarrytown, New York 10591-9001

© Marshall Cavendish Corporation 1997

Library of Congress Cataloging-in-Publication Data
King, David C.
    Egypt: ancient traditions, modern hopes / by David C. King.
        p.   cm. — (Exploring cultures of the world)
    Summary: Discusses the geography, history, culture, daily life, and people of the North African country of Egypt.
    ISBN 0-7614-0142-3 (lib. bdg.)
    1. Egypt—Civilization—Juvenile literature. [1. Egypt.] I. Title. II. Series.
DT170.K56   1997
932—dc21
                                                       96-49588
                                                         CIPxx
                                                            AC

Printed in Hong Kong

Series design by Carol Matsuyama

Front cover: Imbabah Camel Market, Cairo
Back cover: Felucca on the Nile at sunset

Photo Credits
Front cover and pages 34, 41: ©Michael Lichter/International Stock Photo; back cover and pages 17, 57: ©Egyptian Tourist Authority; title page and page 48: ©Klaus Jost/Peter Arnold, Inc.; page 6: Jonathan S. Blair/National Geographic Image Collection; page 11: ©Steve Kaufman/Peter Arnold, Inc.; pages 12, 22, 32, 36, 44, 46: ©Jeffrey L. Rotman/Peter Arnold, Inc.; pages 13, 26: ©Y. Arthus-Bertrand/Peter Arnold, Inc.; page 14: Thomas J. Abercrombie/©National Geographic Society; pages 15, 56: ©Hilary Wilkes/International Stock Photo; page 18: ©Archive Photos; page 20: ©Robert C. Gildart/Peter Arnold, Inc.; page 25: David S. Boyer/©National Geographic Society; pages 28–29: ©David Cimino/International Stock Photo; page 30: ©Erika Stone/Peter Arnold, Inc.; pages 31, 50, 53: ©Winfield I. Parks Jr./National Geographic Image Collection; page 35: ©Tompix/Peter Arnold, Inc.; pages 39, 52: ©George F. Mobley/National Geographic Image Collection; page 42: ©Hartwell/SABA; page 49: O. Louis Mazzatenta/National Geographic Image Collection; page 55: ©J.G. Edmanson/International Stock Photo

Contents

The bustling city of Alexandria, where Egypt's first president, Gamal Abdel Nasser, grew up.

1

GEOGRAPHY AND HISTORY

Egypt Then and Now

The Lion of Egypt

On a blistering hot day in the summer of 1932, there was trouble in the streets of Cairo, the capital of Egypt. A band of young men and boys was marching through the streets to protest the presence of British troops. They wanted the British to leave Egypt so that Egyptians could govern themselves as they saw fit.

There was a scuffle with the police. One of the tallest demonstrators, a teenager, was struck in the forehead. This left a deep scar that he would bear for the rest of his life.

The boy was fourteen-year-old Gamal Abdel Nasser. In later years, he would sometimes touch that scar as if to remind himself how he had received it.

This was not the first time that young Gamal had been in trouble because he opposed British control, and it would not be the last. Though he was raised in the city of Alexandria, Gamal became aware of the terrible poverty of Egypt's peasants, the fellahin. He watched them toil long hours on farmland they could not own, while wealthy landowners relaxed in elegant city clubs miles away. Nasser, who came from a poor family himself, became convinced that the lives of the fellahin and other Egyptians would never improve until the British were driven out of the country.

Despite his occasional troubles with the authorities, Nasser was a good student. He finished secondary school, studied law for a time, and then enrolled in the Royal Military Academy. He was a big, powerfully built young man. Although he was quiet, he had the kind of personality that drew others to him.

In the 1940s, while a lieutenant in the Egyptian Army, Nasser met other young officers who shared his patriotism. They wanted Egypt to be independent, and they wanted to remove the corrupt government of King Farouk. In hopes of doing this, Nasser formed a secret group called the Free Officers. He made sure that no one but himself knew the names of those who had joined.

On July 23, 1952, Nasser and his fellow Free Officers went into action. They quickly and quietly took control of the army. This gave them control of the country. Their revolution was so well planned that neither the Egyptian government officials nor the British had time to react. The secrecy had been so complete that nearly a year passed before the world knew that the man behind the revolution was Colonel Gamal Abdel Nasser.

Some of the Free Officers wanted to execute King Farouk and his ministers. Nasser, however, insisted that the revolution be carried out without violence. "My study of history has taught me that nothing can come of bloodshed but more bloodshed," he said.

After more than 2,000 years of rule by one foreign power after another, Egypt was finally free. Named the country's leader, the young man with the scar on his forehead could now try to fulfill his dream of a better life for the Egyptian people. Over the next seventeen years, he was to become one of the most popular heroes in the nation's history, the man people called the "Lion of Egypt."

A Great River in a Sea of Sand

Astronauts orbiting the earth in a spacecraft can easily identify Egypt: a square patch of brown in the northeast corner of Africa, with a thin green ribbon running through it. The brown coloring is created by the deserts that cover 96 percent of the country. The green is the valley of the Nile River, the longest river in the entire world. The Egyptian portion of the Nile is only the final leg of the mighty river's journey of 4,000 miles (6,400 kilometers) from its source in the mountains of central Africa. From Lake Nasser on Egypt's southern border, the Nile winds north for almost 800 miles (1,280 kilometers). It then spreads into a fan-shaped delta, or mouth, with branches flowing into the Mediterranean Sea.

The Nile River, shown here at Aswan, runs through Egypt from south to north. Its valley provides rich soil for farming.

Except for the Nile Valley and Delta, Egypt is a land of fierce deserts. East of the Nile lies the Eastern Desert. It is a dry, rocky plateau—a high, flat area—that reaches to the Red Sea. Part of this inhospitable region is the Sinai Peninsula, a triangle of rock and sand that points like an arrow into the Red Sea. The Suez Canal links the Red Sea with the Mediterranean Sea. The barren landscape of the Eastern Desert is crisscrossed with dry river beds called wadis (WAH-deez). They turn into raging torrents of water when the occasional rainstorm strikes.

To the west of the Nile stretches the Western Desert. It is part of the massive Sahara Desert, a vast ocean of burning sands and shifting dunes. It has several areas that drop well below sea level. Years may pass between rainfalls in this harsh land, with scorching heat during the day giving way to bitter cold at night. The Western Desert is so parched that no wadis form; the rare rains simply soak into the sand.

The Gift of the Nile

Without the Nile River, Egypt would be a completely barren land. But a special feature of the Nile is that it floods its banks, leaving a rich, dark soil for farming. The fertile valley of the river has made it possible for people to live there for thousands of years. In fact, the Nile River allowed the people of Egypt to develop one of the world's earliest civilizations. Nowhere else on our planet have the people of a country depended so completely on a single geographic feature.

The Nile Valley and Delta cover only 4 percent of the country's area. But this is where nearly all of the people live—99 percent. This means that about 60 million people live in an area smaller than the state of West Virginia! In

Rocks jut from the scorching sands to meet the sky on the Sinai Peninsula.

the desert regions of Egypt, you could travel for days without seeing a settlement or even another human being. And yet parts of Egypt are among the most crowded places on earth.

Egypt's farm villages, towns, and cities are clustered along the Nile and in the Nile Delta, with a few communities scattered along the sea coasts. Cairo, the capital, located on the southern edge of the Delta, is one of the world's largest and most crowded cities. The next-largest city, Alexandria, is a Mediterranean seaport.

In the Eastern Desert, people live in several fishing villages and mining camps along the Red Sea coast. There are also a few groups of Bedouins, who herd camels, sheep, and goats. They move from place to place seeking pasture or water. Because they move so often, they are called nomads.

A Bedouin girl in the Egyptian desert cradles a baby goat.

Sprinkled throughout the Western Desert are a number of places where underground water bubbles to the surface, creating the amazing desert oases. We often think of an oasis as a handful of palm trees surrounded by sand, but a true oasis is surprisingly large. Siwah, the largest of Egypt's oases, has about 15,000 people and has been settled for more than 4,000 years! Siwah has several lakes. It is most famous for the harvests from its many date palms and olive trees.

Farmers dry dates harvested from palm trees. Seen from high above, this oasis south of Cairo makes a colorful patchwork quilt.

These harvests are helped along by the hot sun. The almost endless sunshine is the most striking feature of Egypt's climate. There are only two seasons—winter and summer.

The Land of the Pharaohs

The history of Egypt dates back more than 5,000 years. In about 3100 B.C., a powerful ruler united two kingdoms— Upper Egypt in the south and Lower Egypt in the north. The rulers of this unified kingdom took the title of pharaoh (FAIR-oh), a word that meant "great, or royal, house." For the next 3,000 years, Egypt prospered. It became a very advanced civilization. The contributions of this great culture

This beautiful wall painting of a Nile River scene and hieroglyphics was found in the tomb of Sennefer, the mayor of Thebes some 3,500 years ago.

provided the building blocks for later civilizations throughout Europe and Africa.

Many of the achievements of the ancient Egyptians grew out of their dependence on the Nile. They developed a system of irrigation, for example, to water their fields. Through irrigation, they could trap some of the river's floodwaters in basins. That water was then carried to farms in canals. Egyptians invented one of the first systems of writing, using symbols and figures, called hieroglyphics. This enabled them to keep accurate records about their lives. They also discovered a way to use papyrus—reeds that grow in the marshes of the Nile River—to create the earliest form of paper.

The need to predict exactly when the Nile would flood each year led to the development of astronomy. By studying the courses of the planets and stars, the Egyptians developed a calendar dividing the year into twelve months and 365 days. Our modern calendar is based on this model. The ancient Egyptians also made important advances in mathematics.

Some of ancient Egypt's most remarkable achievements were in architecture and engineering, especially in designing and building the great pyramids. During the Age of the Pyramids, from 2700 to 2200 B.C., more than seventy of these "Houses of Eternity" were constructed. Each pyramid was a monument to the greatness of a pharaoh and a storehouse for the belongings he would need in the afterlife. These included the deceased pharaoh's body, which was preserved through the Egyptians' amazing science of mummification.

The most impressive of the pyramids are at Giza, especially the largest—the Great Pyramid of Cheops. Modern scientists are still trying to determine exactly how a people with no machines, without even iron tools or the wheel,

The massive Sphinx (left) *and Great Pyramid of Cheops dominate the landscape on the Giza Plateau.*

could have cut and moved such enormous blocks of stone. The Cheops Pyramid, for example, was built of more than 2 million perfectly cut blocks, many of them weighing 15 tons (14 metric tons). The stones in the Cheops Pyramid alone could create a wall 10 feet (3 meters) high that would stretch from New York to California!

Twenty-Five Centuries of Foreign Rule

After 2,000 years of greatness, the rule of the pharaohs grew weaker. The wealthy kingdom became an easy target for invading armies. For a few centuries, one foreign power after another gained control of Egypt. These invaders included the Assyrians, Persians, Greeks, and Romans.

The conquerors included some of history's most famous names. Alexander the Great, for example, established Greek rule in Egypt in 332 B.C. His city, Alexandria, became the center of learning and culture for the entire Mediterranean world. Three centuries later, the last Greek ruler, Queen Cleopatra, was defeated by a Roman. More recent invaders included the French conqueror Napoleon Bonaparte in 1798.

In this long parade of invading forces, only a few left a lasting mark on the ancient land. One of them was the Byzantine Empire, which encouraged the spread of Christianity in Egypt in the fourth century A.D. For the next three centuries, Egypt was a Christian country. Today, some Egyptians are members of the Coptic Christian Church.

In A.D. 639, Arab armies from the east brought the new religion of Islam (is-LAM) to Egypt. Not long before, Islam had been founded by the Prophet Muhammad. Soon, the majority of Egyptians had become Muslims (MUZ-limz)—

followers of Islam. They also adopted the Arabic language. It is the official language of Egypt today.

Arab rulers were followed by the Ottoman Turks, who remained in control from 1517 until 1882, except for a brief occupation by the French between 1798 and 1805. One of the rulers of Egypt appointed by the Turks in the early 1800s was a general named Muhammad Ali. Although he ruled as a dictator—a person who has complete power over a country's people—Muhammad Ali did much to modernize Egypt. Under his rule, for example, the people began to grow cotton. It is now one of Egypt's most important products.

Modern Egypt

In 1869, a French company finished building the Suez Canal. This waterway opened a new shipping route between Europe and Asia. Ships could now sail from the Mediterranean Sea through the 100-mile-long (161 kilometers) canal to the Red Sea and the Indian Ocean. They no longer had to make the long journey around the continent of Africa.

A ship steams through the vital Suez Canal.

Great Britain gained control of the Suez Canal in the 1870s. Then, to protect their economic interests, the British decided to take control of Egypt itself.

The Egyptian people were bitterly opposed to British power over their country. In 1922, the British established an Egyptian kingdom, but the king had almost no real power.

Resentment against the British and the weak king led to revolution on July 23, 1952. On that day, Colonel Gamal Abdel Nasser led Egypt to independence. Nasser later became president. His rise to power marked the first time in 2,500 years that Egypt was free of foreign powers.

Gamal Abdel Nasser freed Egypt from foreign control and helped to improve the lives of people.

Nasser ruled Egypt with an iron hand. He allowed no opposition to his rule. However, he also carried out many positive changes that transformed Egypt into a modern nation. Land was taken from the wealthy landowners and given to the fellahin (fela-HEEN), or peasants. Nasser took control of the Suez Canal from the British. He spent the fees paid by users of the canal to improve the country.

One of Nasser's most ambitious projects was the building of the Aswan High Dam. The dam controlled the flow of the Nile and created Lake Nasser, one of the world's largest human-made

EGYPTIAN GOVERNMENT

Egypt is officially called a republic, a form of government in which the authority belongs to the people. Most power in Egypt, however, lies in the hands of its president. Egypt's president today is Hosni Mubarak.

The government has three branches—executive, legislative, and judicial. The executive branch is headed by the president, who appoints a vice president and cabinet. The president serves for a six-year term and may be re-elected to additional terms. All Egyptians have the right to vote once they turn eighteen years of age.

The legislature, or lawmaking body, is the People's Assembly. Of its members, 448 are elected by the people. Another ten members are appointed by the president. Members of the People's Assembly serve for five-year terms and must include some women.

A new Constitution, approved in 1971, established a judicial branch. It is independent of the other two branches of government. The Supreme Constitutional Court is the highest court in the nation.

lakes. Instead of the unpredictable and sometimes damaging yearly floods, the river's water could now be released at a steady rate. This has allowed Egyptian farmers to double the number of crops they can raise. The dam also generates electricity. Almost all rural communities now have some electrical power. Nasser's changes also included building schools and roads, improving health care, establishing new industries, and recognizing the rights of women. Today, long after his sudden death in 1970, he is remembered as the man who taught Egyptians to hope for the future.

Anwar al-Sadat and Hosni Mubarak, the men who followed Nasser as president, continued his reforms. In 1979, Egypt was the first Arab nation to sign a peace treaty with Israel, its longtime enemy. Today, the big challenge that faces Egypt's leaders is to build greater prosperity for the nation's growing population.

This Egyptian of Nubian descent is the captain of a swift felucca.

2

THE PEOPLE

Meet the Egyptians

Visitors to Egypt are often struck by the slow, easygoing pace of life. Egyptians seem to take everything in stride—usually with a sense of humor. The long history of the country, combined with the slow, steady flow of the Nile, seem to create the feeling that there is no need to rush. People stand in line in government offices for hours, or sit in the endless Cairo traffic jams, without becoming upset.

This good-natured patience has been a source of strength to Egypt's people. This same quality can, however, be a source of frustration for those who are trying to introduce new ideas or new technology. Some Egyptians are reluctant to change. The fellahin sometimes will say, "The old ways have worked for so long, why should we bother to change?"

Who Are the Egyptians?

During the centuries when the pharaohs ruled the land, the physical appearance of the slender, tan-skinned Egyptians changed little. But in the centuries that followed, each new foreign invasion led to a mixing of peoples. The majority of Egyptians today represent a blending of the original Egyptians with various Arab groups. Other outside groups—Persian, Greek, Roman, Turkish, and European—added to the mixing of ethnic backgrounds. However, most Egyptians consider themselves to be Arabs. Even the taller, darker-skinned Nubian people of the southern part of Egypt represent a blending of Arab and African.

Arabic is the written and spoken language of Egypt. Arabs everywhere can read what is called "classical" Arabic, but the spoken language differs from place to place. An Arab from the nearby country of Syria or Saudi Arabia can

In front of the family tents, a Bedouin woman cares for her baby.

SAY IT IN ARABIC

Here is how you would say some common words and phrases in Egyptian Arabic:

Good morning.	*Sabah el khair.* (sa-BAH el KHAIR)
Goodbye.	*Ma salama.* (MA sa-LA-ma)
Please.	*Min fadlek.* (min FAD-lek)
Thank you.	*Shukran.* (SHU-kran)
How are you?	*Izzayak.* (iz-ZAY-ak)
I speak English.	*Ana bahki Ingleezi.* (ana BAH-ki in-GLEEZ-i)
What is your name?	*Ismak ay.* (IS-mak AY)
My name is…	*Ismi…* (IS-mi…)
Yes.	*Aiwa.* (AI-wa)
No.	*La.* (LA)
No problem.	*Ma feesh mushkila.* (ma feesh mush-KI-la)

When Egyptians meet, one person usually says, *Salamm alaykum* (sa-LAM a-LAY-kum)—"Peace be upon you." The other replies, *Wa alaykum as-salamm* (WA a-LAY-kum as-sa-LAM)— "And upon you be peace."

read a Cairo newspaper, but would have trouble understanding a taxi driver from Cairo. Most of the scattered tribespeople of the deserts and oases are Bedouin Arabs. They speak a dialect of Arabic.

The Coptic language, which grew out of ancient Egyptian, is now used only in the Coptic Christian Church. Many of the Nubian Egyptians speak a language called Kenuzi. Meanwhile, small minorities of people speak such languages as Italian, Greek, and Armenian.

Village Life

About half of Egypt's people live in the country, in farming villages along the Nile or in the Delta. In some ways, the lives of the fellahin seem unchanged from the way their ancestors lived hundreds, or even thousands, of years ago. Their houses, which are made of mud bricks mixed with straw, are clustered together on dusty, unpaved streets. Men work their fields with ancient-looking plows and, perhaps, a lumbering water buffalo. They lift buckets of water from the irrigation canals with a pole-and-rope device called a shadoof.

In many ways, though, village life has undergone great changes since the 1952 Revolution. The land reform started by Gamal Abdel Nasser, for example, has been one of the most successful agricultural programs in the world. Today, even poor fellahin can own their own plots of land instead of working for others.

The Aswan Dam, completed in 1970, has also brought dramatic changes to the villages. Farmers are no longer dependent on the yearly flooding of the Nile. Since the dam releases water from Lake Nasser at a steady rate, farm families can grow at least two crops each year, and sometimes they grow three or four crops. In summer, the fields of the Delta turn snowy white, as the fellahin devote most of their land to growing cotton. Egyptian cotton is considered to be among the finest in the world. Sales of some of the crop to other countries provide Egypt with an important source of income. The rest of the crop is used in the nation's growing textile industry.

Winter crops include corn, wheat, sugarcane, potatoes, and onions. Farmers also grow a variety of fruits, such as lemons, oranges, melons, mangoes, and dates. Villagers

Bright flowers are cultivated next to the Aswan Dam.

around Lake Nasser can also earn their living by freshwater fishing, and some find work at the government-operated fish farms.

Electricity generated by the Aswan Dam has also transformed rural areas. There is now electric lighting, and most villagers own at least one radio. Nearly every village coffeehouse—a center of community activity—has a television set.

25

Most villagers are farmers. The larger villages also have shopowners, craftspeople, and often a doctor or a lawyer. A growing number of new building complexes have been set up by the government near the larger towns. These are called "service units." They are made up of government offices, a school, an agricultural extension service, and a health clinic. The job of the service units is to help the people. For example, they bring fresh water to the village. They also teach people how to avoid diseases carried by the water of the river and canals.

In the Nile Delta, a group of fellahin work together to harvest the high-quality Egyptian cotton.

THE DESERT NOMADS

Only a few tribes of nomads continue to move with their camels, sheep, and goats from one area of pasture to another. These desert wanderers are fiercely independent. They feel greater loyalty to their small clan groups and larger tribes than to the nation of Egypt. They manage to survive in their harsh environment through trade with people in the fishing villages and mining camps of the Eastern Desert and in the oases of the Western Desert. The nomads provide the townspeople with meat, milk, and wool. In return, they receive tools and utensils, cloth, coffee and tea, spices, and fresh fruits and vegetables.

Oasis Life

Life in the five major oases of the Western Desert has changed more slowly than life in the villages. In some oasis towns, for example, women rarely appear in public. Camels and donkeys are still the main way to get around. But some changes are happening. Schools are being built and roads are being paved. The government has plans to expand several of the oases to make room for families from the crowded villages in the Nile Valley.

Life in the City

In Cairo, a visitor can sit in a revolving, glass-walled restaurant high atop Cairo Tower and gaze down on a city of contrasts. Modern office buildings, apartment complexes, and hotels rise above ancient buildings on narrow, winding streets and alleyways. Cars and trucks clog the streets, often competing for space with a donkey cart or a string of camels. Prosperous businesspeople in modern Western-style clothing walk past robed beggars sitting cross-legged on straw mats. Women wearing the latest Paris and New York fashions mingle with women covered from head to toe with Egypt's traditional black cloaks, called *melayas*.

On a cliff in central Cairo, a massive twelfth-century fortress called the Citadel looms over the city. Rising above the Citadel are the towers of a mosque (mahsk)—a Muslim

The Cairo skyline reveals Egypt's fascinating blend of buildings, both old and new.

house of worship. This holy place was built less than 200 years ago. Not far from the fortress are the narrow, twisting alleys of Khan el-Khalil Bazaar. Egypt's colorful marketplaces, or souks (sooks), are all called bazaars. Khan el-Khalil is a crowded maze of family-owned shops that make and sell a dazzling array of goods. There are beautifully carved wooden boxes, intricate brass lanterns, silk shawls, lace table-cloths, and endless trays of gold and silver jewelry. The air

Traffic-clogged streets are a common sight in Cairo.

is heavy with the scent of coffee, spices, and perfumes.

Cairo, like Egypt's other cities, is very crowded. The Egyptians clearly need more living space. To achieve this, the government has started a program of building satellite towns—new urban centers, with their own businesses and government services.

How well a family lives in the city depends largely on its income. Office workers and professional people usually live in apartment houses. Many now have air conditioning, and there is a balcony for every apartment. Sitting outdoors in the evening has been a favorite pastime throughout Egypt's history.

The cities also have many poor people. Most have homes, even if these are nothing more than a tin shack or a mud hut. But there are also thousands of homeless people, especially in Cairo. They often sleep on mats in alleys or on rooftops.

Religion and the Rhythm of Life

Every day at noon, the bustling streets of Cairo come to a standstill as a voice over a loudspeaker calls out, "Allah [God] is most great! There is no God but Allah! Come to prayer! Come to salvation!" The words are called out from the balcony of a minaret—the tall, slender tower of a mosque—by an official known as a muezzin (moo-EZ-zin).

All devout Muslims stop whatever they are doing to heed this call to prayer. Whether in mosques or in the street, they kneel down to pray, foreheads touching the ground and facing the direction of the holy city of Mecca (in Saudi Arabia). The call to prayer is repeated five times a day in every village, town, and city.

Faithful Muslims kneel in prayer outside a mosque at sunset.

The great majority of the Egyptian people are Muslims. Their religion is woven into the daily pattern of their lives. Most go to a mosque on Friday, the Muslim holy day. Nearly everyone also fasts during daylight hours in the month of Ramadan. Religion affects how people live in many other ways. Devout Muslims, for example, do not gamble, eat pork, or drink alcohol.

Most other Egyptians are Coptic Christians. In addition, there are some Roman Catholics, Protestants, and Jews.

A young Bedouin woman wears a traditional wedding veil.

3
FAMILY LIFE, FESTIVALS, AND FOOD

Tradition and Change

In some Egyptian families, women spend most of their time in the home. When they do go out, they completely cover their hair with a black headdress. In other families, though, especially in the cities, women may dress in brightly colored clothes as they go off to work in shops, offices, or factories. Everywhere in Egypt there is a contrast between older ways of life and newer lifestyles.

Whether traditional or modern, every Egyptian family is closely knit. A holiday meal usually includes not just parents and children but also cousins, aunts, uncles, and grandparents. In families with mothers working outside the home, children are cared for by relatives rather than by babysitters or day-care centers. Older sons and daughters usually live at home until they marry. In the past few years, however, a growing number of young people have traveled to other countries to look for jobs.

These parents and their children, dressed in traditional clothing, enjoy a walk through a bazaar in Cairo.

New Roles for Women and Children

In Egypt, educational and job opportunities for women have grown steadily. Today, nearly a third of the students in Egypt's universities are women. More and more women have careers as nurses and doctors, lawyers, teachers, scientists, and other professions that require advanced education.

Families in which both parents work tend to have fewer children than others. Among the fellahin, families continue to have five, six, or more children. In the past, large families were important. More children meant that farmers had more help in the fields. The children were also expected to take care of their parents in their old age.

The tendency toward large families is changing, however. This is true even in the farming communities. All Egyptian children today are required to go to school for at least six years. This limits the amount of farm work they can do.

34

Parents today also believe that education is the way to a better life for their children. If the family is kept small, there is a better chance that the children will be able to complete secondary school and perhaps go on to college.

A Daily Pattern

An Egyptian family's day begins early. Businesses open at 8:00 or 9:00 A.M., and the school day starts at the same time. The school and work week begins on Saturday or Sunday and ends on Thursday. Schools and most businesses are closed on Friday to observe the weekly Muslim holy day.

The main reason for the early start to the day is Egypt's midday heat. Almost everything closes in the early afternoon, and most people go home for a few hours, until the worst of the heat has passed. Businesses then re-open until 8:00 or 9:00 P.M.

Egyptians usually go to the market every day. They like to eat lots of fresh fruit and vegetables.

The pattern of the day helps to maintain close family ties. Since most people return home for the afternoon, family members usually gather together and enjoy their main meal. At the end of the day, they have a light evening meal or a snack.

People tend to stay up late because they have slept, or at least rested, during the afternoon. Families often spend the evening sitting on their balconies or taking a long walk. Movies are also popular, with most starting around 9:00 P.M. Restaurants and coffeehouses stay open well past midnight.

Holy Days, Holidays, and Festivals

The midday meal is an important social event for most Egyptian families. This meal is even more special on festival days. On those days, most people have the day off from school and work. The family may spend the entire afternoon around the table. The delicious meal is likely to be followed by games, singing, or a visit from relatives or friends.

The most solemn holy days in the Muslim religion occur during the month of Ramadan. Ramadan is observed

Bedouins in the Sinai Peninsula share an evening meal during Ramadan.

MEALS AND MANNERS

When friends or relatives visit an Egyptian family, the guests are offered tiny cups of strong, sweet Turkish coffee. The guests always accept, because it is impolite to refuse. In fact, they will usually take a second or third cup to show they appreciate the family's hospitality. If the guests bring a gift, it is received either with both hands or the right hand—but never the left.

During the meal, "finger food" is eaten only with the right hand. In most rural areas, all food is eaten as finger food. The use of knives and forks is rare. In cities and towns, though, these utensils are used European-style, with the knife remaining in the right hand and the fork in the left.

At the end of the meal, polite guests always leave a little food on their plates. Leftovers are a sign of abundance. Leaving some food shows appreciation for the great feast the family has prepared.

according to the Islamic calendar, which follows the phases of the moon, rather than the solar calendar most Westerners are familiar with. Because of this, the Muslim holy month occurs at a different time each year.

Ramadan celebrates the month when Allah revealed Himself to the Prophet Muhammad, the founder of Islam, in the seventh century A.D. Muslims think about ways that they can improve themselves and come closer to the teachings of the Koran, the Muslim holy book.

Throughout Ramadan, people have nothing to eat or drink during the daylight hours. The fast begins exactly at dawn, when a white thread can first be distinguished from a black thread. When it is too dark to tell the threads apart, the day's fast ends. Fasting is especially hard during the summer. This is one time when Egyptians are likely to lose some of their characteristic good humor.

As soon as it is dark, Muslims have a hearty meal called *iftar* (if-TAR)—"breaking the fast." After the meal, there is a short prayer. Family members then spend time in quiet thought. Everyone gets up before dawn to enjoy a meal that will keep them going through another long day of fasting.

Ramadan ends with a three-day holiday called *Aid al Fitr*. This is a joyous time when special meals are prepared and people exchange gifts with friends and relatives.

Other Muslim holy days are also celebrated during the year. The Prophet Muhammad's birthday is celebrated as a festival. Every city and large town sets up a carnival. There are Ferris wheels, merry-go-rounds, and people selling snacks and souvenirs. Since this holy day follows the lunar calendar, it is observed at a different time each year.

Egyptians also celebrate several national holidays, using the Western, or solar, calendar. Labor Day (May 1), the Anniversary of the Revolution (July 23), and Armed Forces Day (October 6) are patriotic holidays, much like the Fourth of July in the United States. Another time for celebration is a spring festival, *Sham el-Nasseem*, which means "The Scent of the Breeze." This holiday is an occasion to welcome spring, usually with a family picnic.

What's for Dinner?

Preparations for the midday meal are usually very complex, especially if guests have been invited. On holidays or feast days, the meal may last for hours.

A meal often starts with an appetizer such as peanuts, followed by pasta. The main course is usually a roast chicken or kebabs—small chunks of lamb, heavily spiced and broiled on skewers. Beef is expensive, so it is eaten rarely. Pork or ham is never served because eating the meat of a pig is forbidden by Islam. Seafood is another popular main dish,

At their home on an Egyptian oasis, a mother and daughter mix dough for the afternoon meal.

especially red snapper and giant prawns. The meat or seafood is accompanied by yellow saffron rice and stuffed grape leaves. There may also be a stuffed-vegetable dish called *mahshi*. Everything is generously seasoned with spices and oil, and there is always plenty of fresh-baked bread.

After the main course comes a variety of fresh fruits, such as dates, grapes, melons, mangoes, bananas, and oranges. The most popular dessert is baklava—layers of flaky pastry and chopped nuts and honey. Adults drink plenty of thick, sweet Turkish coffee or glasses of mint-flavored tea, also served very sweet. Children usually drink *ayran*, a zesty beverage made of yogurt and water.

ANCIENT-DAY SALAD

1 large cucumber	2 teaspoons lemon juice
1 cup (1/2 pint) plain yogurt	Dash of salt and pepper
1 teaspoon dill	3 sprigs fresh mint leaves

Peel the cucumber and dice it. Put the cucumber, yogurt, dill, and lemon juice into a mixing bowl and stir until well mixed. Season the mixture to your taste with salt and pepper. Place it in a serving bowl. Top it with fresh chopped mint (if available)—do not use dried mint. Cover it with plastic wrap and chill it for 10 minutes in the refrigerator or until you are ready to serve it.

The most common food for the light evening meal or snack is falafel. Chickpeas are boiled and crushed, mixed with parsley and spices, shaped into balls, and fried in oil. Then they are stuffed into flat bread with sliced tomatoes and pickled vegetables. They make a most tasty snack.

Clothing: Traditional and Modern

The clothing people wear reflects Egypt's blending of the modern with older ways. In cities modern styles are common. Men wear business suits or shirts and trousers, and women wear dresses.

Even in the cities, however, many people continue to wear the traditional clothing that is common in rural areas. Men wear a long tunic called a *galabia*, with white cotton trousers or short pants underneath. On their heads, some men wear turbans, others a skullcap. The fez—a red, pillbox-type Turkish cap—is rarely worn. The traditional dress for women is the long, hooded *melaya*. Rural women, and especially the women of the oases, celebrate festival days with lots of jewelry, including beautiful necklaces, bracelets, and rings.

This boy's robe is similar to those worn by his ancestors for many generations.

Among Egyptians, whether traditional or modern, the key word in clothing is modesty. Even in the cities, for example, young women in brightly colored cotton dresses may cover their hair. And only the most modern of women would appear in public with short sleeves.

In Egyptian schools, girls and boys sit apart, even if they are in the same classroom. These girls are in a school in Cairo.

4

SCHOOL AND RECREATION

In School and Out

Until recently, formal education was almost completely ignored in Egypt. The few schools that did exist were devoted largely to the study of the Koran. Boys—no girls were allowed—learned the Muslim holy book by chanting its poetic phrases over and over. In addition to these Koranic schools, wealthy Egyptians could send their children to private schools operated by foreign groups, such as missionaries. Not surprisingly, only about one adult in ten could read and write.

In the 1920s, a law was passed declaring that all children must attend school from seven to twelve years of age. But no one paid any attention to the law. There were no school buildings, no trained teachers, and no books.

When Nasser came to power after the 1952 Revolution, he was determined to bring education to all Egyptians. The government began building schools, training teachers, and printing textbooks. The number of schools multiplied rapidly. Soon, schools could be found even in farm villages and oases. Today, nearly all Egyptian children attend primary school, beginning when they are six years old. Education is free for everyone, right through secondary school and college.

Outdoor exercise is an important part of the school day at this school in the Egyptian countryside.

The Egyptian people know that it will take time to overcome the years of neglect, but they are proud of the progress they are making. About half of today's adults can read and write. That amount will rise as today's children grow up.

Opportunities to Learn

About 80 percent of Egyptian children are now finishing all six years of primary school. In their last year, the children take a nationwide exam. Those who do well are invited to go on to three years of preparatory school. That is much like a junior high school in the United States. The fifteen-year-olds who complete the three years take another set of tests to see who will continue on for three years of secondary school.

There are two types of secondary school. One type, called a general school, offers academic subjects similar to those in American high schools. The other type, technical school, provides job training for work in agriculture, business, or industry. There are also special schools attached to al-Azhar University in Cairo, the oldest and most important school devoted to the study of Islam.

The hardest tests of all are the exams for entrance into one of the thirteen universities in Egypt. Only a small percentage of young people now go this far. However, the universities are training a growing number of people, who find jobs in such fields as medicine, law, and education.

School Days

Imagine that you are a primary-school student living in a small village on the banks of the Nile. You have to be up early, because the school day starts at 7:00 A.M. A ten-minute bus ride along the glistening waters of the river takes you to a government "service unit." The cluster of new brick buildings houses your school, a health clinic, and classrooms for adults who want to learn to read and write.

There are thirty-four students in your class. Your teacher is a young woman who recently graduated from Cairo University. Since books are scarce, you spend much of your time writing with chalk on small slates.

For the first two years of primary school, the daily lessons are in reading, writing, and some arithmetic. In the third year, science and study of the Koran are added. In the fourth year, students begin to learn a foreign language. Most students study English as their foreign language. Some private schools offer French, Russian, and German as well.

Learning a foreign language presents two tricky adjustments. First, alphabets in other languages are very different from the 28 characters used in Arabic. The second difficulty is that most other languages, like English, are read from left to right, while Arabic moves from right to left.

Many students will not go beyond the primary grades, so the schools offer practical subjects that will help them as working adults. Girls take classes in cooking, sewing, and embroidery. Boys learn about farming or how to work with leather and metal.

The government and the people are trying hard to bring education up to date. But the task is difficult, because the population is growing so fast. More and more children enter the schools each year, creating serious crowding and shortages of supplies. In fact, in your school in the service unit, you might be dismissed for the day at noon so that another class can use the room in the afternoon.

The Egyptian people realize how important education is. In rural villages, where many homes still lack electric lights, it is not unusual to see groups of students studying under the village street lamps. And, in the cities, many families hire

Through books, this child can learn about places far away from the dry Egyptian desert.

COMIC RELIEF

Egyptians are known for their sense of humor and their fondness for silly jokes and stories. Their favorite comic figure is a make-believe character named Nasrudin. Nasrudin always does things backward. In cartoons, he even rides his donkey backward. The reason, he says, is that he wants to see where he's going, and the donkey never goes where he tells it to. A typical Nasrudin story goes like this:

A friend saw Nasrudin on his hands and knees under a lamppost. When asked what he was doing, Nasrudin explained that he was looking for his keys.

"Do you know where you lost them?" the friend asked.

"Yes," Nasrudin replied. "I lost them in the house."

"Then why are you looking for them out here?"

"Because the light is better!"

special tutors to help their children prepare for the examinations. The government also offers rewards for high scores. Each year, for example, the best students in every school are invited to Cairo for special ceremonies on Independence Day.

As you ride the school bus back to your village, the Nile River looks much as it did thousands of years ago. And the sailboats, called feluccas, moving slowly against the current, also have not changed. But because you are in school, Egypt's future is likely to be very different from its past.

Outdoor Fun

Since Egypt's weather is sunny and warm all year, children spend most of their free time outdoors. On Friday—the day of rest in Muslim countries—the children often go with their families to a public garden or park for a picnic. During the heat of the day, no one moves around much. Then, as the air begins to cool, late in the afternoon, children play games such as tag, hide-and-go-seek, and blindman's bluff. Family gatherings are noisy and joyful. There is a good deal of laughing, singing, and often a practical joke or two.

On the coast, the beaches are always crowded. In the countryside, children shout with glee as they swoop down mud slides into the irrigation canals.

The favorite evening pastime throughout Egypt is a stroll through the streets. Families meet their friends and buy food from sidewalk vendors—fresh fruit, ice cream, soft drinks, and *semeet*, a crusty bread that is similar to pretzels. The strolling families usually watch street performers, especially during festivals or holidays. Musicians, dancers, jugglers, acrobats, magicians, and sometimes even a snake charmer or animal trainer all compete for the attention of the crowds. Men like to sit at tables in front of the many coffeehouses, talking about politics or playing backgammon or dominoes. Because ancient traditions die hard, women still are not welcome in the coffeehouses.

Because the weather is so warm, people in Egypt can enjoy the beach almost every day of the year.

A Growing Interest in Sports

Fifty years ago, there were almost no organized team sports in Egypt. Then the Egyptian people discovered the world of sports, both as players and as spectators. On a weekend today, 100,000 people will cram into Cairo Stadium to watch an important soccer match. Soccer (which is called "football" in Egypt, as in most countries) has become the national sport. It is growing in popularity every year.

There are no professional soccer teams with high-salaried stars in

48

Near Luxor, children play a lively game of soccer.

Egypt. Instead, there are dozens of clubs, whose players have their own uniforms and a loyal following of fans. Television stations carry hours of soccer games, and fans follow their favorite teams closely through newspaper and radio reports.

There are clubs for all major sports. They offer a wide variety of activities, including tennis, swimming, horseback riding, and fishing. Rowing has become popular, especially since a Cairo police officers' club won several races against American college teams. Dozens of scuba clubs have sprung up along the coast of the Red Sea, offering training in scuba diving. The beautiful coral reefs along the coast are teeming with brightly colored tropical fish.

Some sports clubs practice ancient sports, such as wrestling and weightlifting. These sports have a large following during international competitions, especially the Summer Olympic Games. Another popular ancient sport is the racing of purebred Arabian horses, either on tracks or over the sands. Large crowds are always on hand for the weekend races.

These boys are learning how to make a beautiful wall hanging. This craft has been practiced in Egypt for centuries.

5
THE ARTS

Blending the Old
and the New

No country has a longer tradition of great achievement in arts and crafts than Egypt. Millions of visitors from all over the world travel to Egypt to gaze in wonder at the great pyramids and temples and to see magnificent museum collections. And today, Egyptians continue to excel in many artistic areas, including crafts, literature, and the movies.

The Craft Tradition

The craftspeople of Egypt have been producing beautiful handmade objects for thousands of years. In ancient times, the tombs of pharaohs and nobles were filled with lovely sculptures of wood or stone, intricately carved wooden cabinets, wall paintings, and fine jewelry made of gold and semiprecious gems. One of the most amazing relics of ancient Egypt was found in the tomb of Tutankhamen—a chest inlaid with 33,000 tiny pieces of ivory and ebony.

Islam was a powerful influence on Egyptian arts and crafts. Muslim artists were discouraged from using human or animal forms in their works. Instead, they created complex

This souk in Alexandria contains many kinds of handicrafts—from brass trays to embroidered cloths.

patterns of geometric shapes. These pretty shapes were intertwined with vines, leaves, and flowers. This style of design is called arabesque. Arabic writing was also used for decoration because of its graceful, flowing shapes. Any phrases or sentences, however, had to be quotations from the Koran.

Today, in every souk, or bazaar, families of craftspeople build on the great traditions of the past. In one section of the marketplace these artisans hand-tie each knot of richly colored rugs or wall hangings. In other parts of the souk, family workshops produce gold or silver jewelry, embroidered cotton and leather goods. Others make carefully detailed plates, coffeepots, and vases of copper or brass. Some of the items are echoes of ancient times. A souk stall might specialize in jewelry items decorated with hieroglyphics, for example, while another may offer the ancient writing on a papyrus scroll.

Music and Dance

Whenever Egyptian families have a party or celebration, there is likely to be music and dancing. The music is varied, ranging from old Arabic songs to the latest pop and country hits from the United States or Europe. There is also a growing interest in the folk music of the rural villages. Some of the songs are centuries old. One of Egypt's most popular singers and song writers, Muhammad Abd al-Wahhab, blends these folk melodies with rhythms borrowed from Western-style music.

Dance is also varied. For recreational dancing, young people in the cities enjoy the disco-style dances of North America and Europe. Older people tend to prefer Arabic dance—a slower movement, with the feet kept close together. Folk dances, used for centuries in religious festivals, are enjoying a renewed popularity. Two companies of folk dancers, Rida's Troupe and the National Folk Dance Ensemble, draw large crowds everywhere and have performed all over the world.

Musicians perform during a festival in the sacred month of Ramadan.

EGYPT IN ARTS AND LETTERS

Modern Egypt has given the world many wonderful novelists, poets, and musicians. But several names stand out as giants.

One is **Om Kolthum** (1904–1975), Egypt's most beloved singer for more than fifty years. Her songs are both sad and yet somehow hopeful, a mixture of moods that seem to capture the spirit of Egypt. Kolthum is known as the "Mother of Egypt." Her classical Arab melodies are heard every day on Egyptian radio and in people's homes.

Many modern Egyptian writers have explored a common theme: How should their society respond to the power and industrial development of the West (Europe and North America)? Two great novelists who examined this question were **Tawfiq al-Hakim** (1898–1987) in *The Bird from the East* and **Yahya Haqqi** (1905–1992) in a short novel called *The Lamp of Umm Hashim*. Some writers have looked at the effect of the West on the rural areas. Egypt's greatest novelist, **Naguib Mahfouz** (1912–   ), describes the changing way of life in the cities. Mahfouz is the only Egyptian to win the Nobel Prize for Literature. In his most famous book, *Midaq Alley*, he shows an amazing ability to capture the color of life among the poor people of the cities. *Miramar* is the story of a young woman who runs away to Alexandria to escape a marriage arranged by her family. Her relationships with her neighbors in the city give Mahfouz the opportunity to create vivid word portraits of modern life.

A Poetic Tradition

Novels and plays have developed in Egypt only in the past century. Poetry, however, has a long history. Egyptian poets began writing rhymed couplets in Arabic more than 1,000 years ago. The couplets were formed into long poetic stories that told of desert life, great heroic deeds in battle, or a tragic love. Some modern Egyptian poets have followed this historic tradition. Others have expressed themselves through different poetic forms.

Ancient Treasures

Every year, several million tourists travel to Egypt to view some of the world's oldest wonders. The Great Pyramids and the Sphinx at Giza are only the beginning of a 5,000-year journey through artistic history.

Magnificent sculptures, paintings, jewelry, and other items have survived so many centuries for two main reasons. First, they were preserved in tombs. The ancient Egyptians believed that this life was only a brief time before an eternal, or never-ending, "afterlife." Even average people wanted to take their most-treasured possessions on the journey to the afterlife. The great pharaohs, of course, could afford to have their tombs filled with the finest objects that craftworkers could produce. For this reason, most of the great artistic treasures of Egypt have been found in the pyramids and in the Valley of the Tombs of the Kings, near the city of Luxor. The

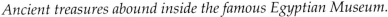

Ancient treasures abound inside the famous Egyptian Museum.

THE TREASURES OF TUTANKHAMEN

The pharaohs of ancient Egypt took great care to have all sorts of secret passageways built into their burial places. However, over the centuries, all of the pyramids and tombs were broken into by tomb robbers. All, that is, except the tomb of King Tut.

In the 1920s, a British archaeologist named Howard Carter became convinced that not all of the tombs had been discovered. For years, he searched in vain through the Valley of the Tombs of the Kings, near the modern city of Luxor. Then, one day in 1922, he and his workers found a stone door hidden by the sands. Carter carefully poked a small hole through the door and looked in.

The golden death mask of Tutankhamen.

"Can you see anything?" the expedition leader asked.

"Yes," the awestruck Carter answered. "Wonderful things!"

What Carter had found was the tomb of Tutankhamen, or King Tut. He was a young pharaoh who died around 1330 B.C. In one chamber after another carved out of rock, Carter found chests, stools, couches, and dozens of other items. Everything seemed to be plated in gold, even the walls of the burial chamber.

The tomb held not only great wealth but some of the finest wall paintings and most beautiful objects ever found in one place. The immense treasure was moved to the Egyptian Museum. Eventually, after it had been studied, the mummified body of the young king was returned to its original resting place.

These huge stone figures at Abu Simbel remind visitors of Egypt's long and glorious history.

second reason why these works have survived is Egypt's climate. It is so dry that it slows the decay of cloth, wood, and other materials.

Egypt has many museums and ancient buildings. The greatest storehouse of artistic treasures, though, is the Egyptian Museum. The museum's 100,000 items include statues in stone and wood, and beautifully carved furniture. There are wall paintings of scenes of daily life in realistic colors, and a wide array of finely crafted jewels.

Egypt's ancient splendors do not stop with the treasures of the pharaohs. Alexandria has rich collections from Greek and Roman times. Cairo contains some of the finest examples of Islamic architecture, especially in the city's many mosques.

Country Facts

Official Name: Jumhuriyuh Misr al-Arabiya (Arab Republic of Egypt)

Capital: Cairo

Location: Egypt is located in the northeast corner of Africa. It is bordered by the Mediterranean Sea on the north; the Red Sea forms most of the eastern boundary. Only three countries are on Egypt's borders: Libya to the west, Sudan to the south, and Israel to the east.

Area: 386,650 square miles (1,007,258 square kilometers). *Greatest distances:* east–west, 770 miles (1,239 kilometers); north–south, 675 miles (1,087 kilometers). *Coastline:* Mediterranean, 620 miles (1,000 kilometers); Red Sea and Gulf of Aqaba, 1,200 miles (1,920 kilometers)

Elevation: *Highest:* Jabal Katrina (Mount Catherine), in the southern Sinai Peninsula, 8,668 feet (2,643 meters). *Lowest:* Ottara Depression, in the Western Desert, 436 feet (166 meters) below sea level

Climate: Hot and dry. Two seasons: winter, from December to March, 55°–70° F (13°–21° C); summer, from April to November, 80°–90° F (27°–32° C). The Mediterranean coast receives about 7 inches (17.5 centimeters) of rain per year; Cairo 1 inch (2.5 centimeters); deserts and southern Egypt receive almost no rain.

Population: 62,360,000. *Distribution:* 55 percent urban; 45 percent rural

Form of Government: Republic

Important Products: *Natural Resources:* oil, hydroelectric and thermal power, phosphate, manganese, coal. *Agriculture:* cotton, corn, rice, wheat, sugarcane, vegetables and fruits, sheep, camels, goats, cattle, donkeys, water buffalo. *Industries:* iron and steel; aluminum; food processing; cotton clothing and other textiles; tourism

Basic Unit of Money: pound; 1 pound = 33 cents

Language: Arabic

Religion: 92 percent Muslim; 8 percent Coptic Christian, Protestant, Roman Catholic, and Jewish

Flag: Three wide stripes—red for sacrifice, white for purity, black for history—with a golden hawk in the center symbolizing the tribe of Muhammad, the founder of Islam

National Anthem: *Walla Zanan ya Silahi* ("The Time Has Come to Reach for Our Weapons")

Major Holidays: National holidays: Unity Day, February 22; Labor Day, May 1; Independence Day, July 23; Armed Forces Day, October 6. Muslim holidays follow the lunar calendar and therefore vary from year to year: the month of Ramadan, which ends with the three-day *Aid al Fitr*; Muhammad's Birthday; the Muslim New Year; *Sham el-Nasseem* ("The Scent of the Breeze"), a spring festival

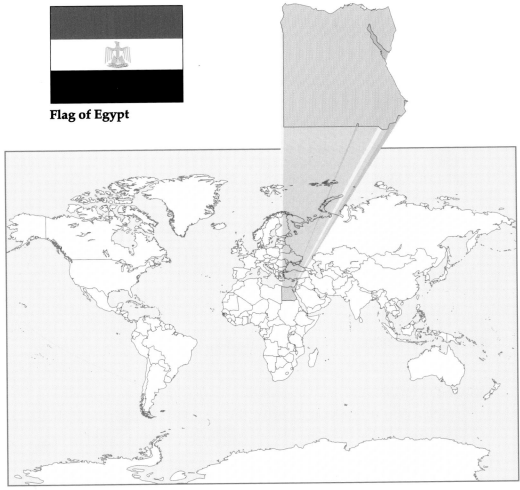

Flag of Egypt

Egypt in the World

Glossary

afterlife: according to some people's beliefs, a life after death

Allah: the word for God in the Arabic language

arabesque: a style of design that uses pretty shapes of leaves and flowers to produce intricate patterns

delta: a fan-shaped area formed by a river as it divides into branches before flowing into the sea

fellahin (fela-HEEN): Egyptian peasants; farmers in rural Egypt

felucca: a small, narrow sailboat that has been in use on the Nile River since the days of the pharaohs

galabia: a long tunic, worn by men, with cotton trousers or short pants underneath

hieroglyphics: one of the world's earliest forms of writing. Egyptian hieroglyphs combined pictures, called pictographs, with symbols.

iftar (if-TAR): a hearty meal that breaks a fast

irrigation: a system of canals and catch basins that allow farmers to water their fields

Islam (is-LAM): a religion founded in the seventh century A.D. by Muhammad. People who follow Islam are **Muslims**. They believe that there is one God, Allah, and that Muhammad is his prophet, or messenger

Koran: the Islamic holy book

melaya: a traditional cloak, usually black, that covers a woman from head to toe

mosque: a Muslim house of worship. Men and women pray separately. When entering a mosque, people remove their shoes and wash their hands.

muezzin (moo-EZ-zin): person who calls Muslims to prayer

mummification: the ancient Egyptian process of preserving human bodies after death. The bodies were embalmed and wrapped in linen. Some mummified bodies have remained intact for more than 3,000 years.

Muslims (MUZ-limz): followers of the religion of Islam. About 94 percent of the Egyptian people are Muslims.

nomads: wandering people who move their livestock from place to place to find fresh pasture and water

oasis: an area in a desert where springs or underground water support plant life. There are five major oases in Egypt's Western Desert.

papyrus: reeds growing in marshy areas of the Nile and other rivers; used by ancient Egyptians to make an early form of paper

pharaoh (FAIR-oh): the title used by the rulers of ancient Egypt.

skullcap: a close-fitting cap without a brim

souk (sook): a marketplace, or bazaar, in North Africa and the Middle East in which a wide variety of goods are sold in small shops and stalls

turban: a head covering made by wrapping a long strip of cloth around the head several times

wadis (WAH-deez): river beds in the desert that are normally dry, except during the occasional rainfall

For Further Reading

Crosher, Judith. *Ancient Egypt.* New York: Viking Press, 1993.

Cross, Wilber. *Egypt.* Chicago: Childrens Press, 1992.

Feinstein, G. *Egypt in Pictures.* Minneapolis, Minnesota: Lerner Publications, 1988.

Harrison, Steve and Patricia. *Egypt: BBC Fact Finders.* London, England: British Broadcasting Corporation, 1990.

Malam, John. *Indiana Jones Explores Ancient Egypt.* Boston: Little, Brown & Co., 1992.

Marston, Elsa. *The Ancient Egyptians.* New York: Marshall Cavendish, 1995.

Parker, Lewis K. *Dropping In On Egypt.* Vero Beach, Florida: Rourke Book Company, 1994.

Pateman, Robert. *Egypt.* New York: Marshall Cavendish, 1993.

Percefull, Aaron W. *The Nile.* New York: Franklin Watts, 1984.

Wilkins, Frances. *Let's Visit Egypt.* London, England: Burke Publishing Company, 1983.

Index

Page numbers for illustrations are in boldface

About the Author

"One of the great things about books is that they can carry us to every corner of the world. We can also travel back in time, visiting people and places from recent years or the distant past. I hope you enjoy this book's journey across both space and time," says David C. King.

Mr. King is a historian and an author, who has written more than thirty books for young readers. In addition to books about foreign countries, he has written stories and biographies in American history. He and his wife, Sharon Flitterman-King, live in the village of Hillsdale, New York. They welcome visitors.